Hattie Howard

Later Poems

Hattie Howard

Later Poems

ISBN/EAN: 9783744705271

Printed in Europe, USA, Canada, Australia, Japan

Cover: Foto ©Thomas Meinert / pixelio.de

More available books at **www.hansebooks.com**

LATER POEMS

BY

HATTIE HOWARD.

———

Books and friends O choose with care!
Lest, deluded by the glare
  Of their covers, or their looks,
You may some day in despair
  Rue your choice of friends and books.

————

HARTFORD, CONN.
1887.

⊹ Contents ⊹

Poems

March.

March, thou month of varied weather!
Mild and frigid joined together —
  " Winter," amorous poets sing,
  " Ling'ring in the lap of Spring."

Full of reckless threat and bluster
Thou, like daring filibuster,
  Will not yield thy fitful way,
  Though a king dispute thy sway.

Month of terror, storm, and blizzard!
Never work of skillful wizard,
  Though in magic unsurpassed,
  Surer, swifter than the last.

Period of expectation!
Link between the desolation
  And the glory of the year —
  Time of roses drawing near.

Monarch viewed in many guises
Giving, as in rare surprises,
    While we stand with cold benumb,
    Hints of balminess to come.

March, like mortals waxing crazy
For the arbutus and daisy,
    Violet and crocus-cup
    Round our pathway springing up.

Timidly the grass is creeping,
Daffodils awake from sleeping,
    And the long-dismantled woods
    Are alive with bursting buds.

Sweetest notes are bluebirds trilling,
Leafless groves with music filling,
    To whose tuneful prophecies
    Every heart responsive is.

Fickle March! from thee we borrow
Rays of promise for the morrow;
    For are coming, soon or late,
    Perfect days — if we but wait.

Generous Giving.

I read of receptions in salons of fashion,
　Of music, militia, and festival bells ;
Of elegant banquets that ravish the palate,
Of beauty, enchantress and queen of the ballet,
　In motion as graceful as dancing gazelles.

I think of Society's doings, and wonder —
　It seems such a foolish and frivolous show —
If ever were deeds of beneficence fewer,
If ever a thought of the life that is truer
　Invaded those beings with tinsel aglow.

Then turn for a moment from glittering splendor,
　And into the hovels of poverty go ;
To meet peradventure the jeweled patrician
Abroad on benevolent, heavenly mission,
　Whose kindness alone its recipients know.

O never again may unworthy reflection
　Thus picture humanity heartless and gay ;
For never was more of spontaneous giving
Or helping to holier, happier living,
　Than brightens the earth to her children to-day.

Yea, hidden by drapery, diamonds, and gilding,
　Do goodness and opulence tenderly keep
A corner of love for the fortune-forsaken,
Of pity for those by adversity shaken,
　A tear for the sad who in solitude weep.

Ambition.

I have not wrought for fame or gold,
    To gain position, praise, or power,
Nor that I might o'er others hold
    The envied vantage of an hour;
For honeyed compliments that lie
    Profuse upon the flatterer's tongue,
Or Fashion's captive butterfly,
    No song of mine was ever sung.

I would not dare to while away
    In aimless, apathetic mood
The precious moments of a day
    Without a care for others' good;
And thus in Love's unmeasured stint
    An undercurrent seems to run —
A wish to bear some helpful hint
    Or bit of cheer to every one.

On each impulsive act or word
    Whatever merit may depend,
Is shown when one, in spirit stirred
    To recognize its honest trend,
Hath been uplifted; and perchance
    In thankfulness and sympathy,
Through lonely space by swift advance
    A cordial hand held out to me.

And so for those who know me true,
   Who've loved me longest, loved me best,
Because of aught that I may do
   In friendly overtures expressed
To brighten Life's short pilgrimage,
   Ambition's aim is gratified;
Though culture, lore, and wisdom sage
   To me forever be denied.

"Ben Hur."

Scion of an illustrious line
   For ages rich in noble blood,
That kept, as 'twere a thing divine,
   Its record clear — beyond the Flood!

What were a haughty rival's boast
   Compared to thine, of ancient home
And ancestry, whose dawn at most
   Coeval was with that of Rome?

Above, not of, the populace!
   Born to a prince's proud estate;
But driven from thy rightful place
   By harsh vicissitudes of Fate.

Long service at the galley-oar
   Thy kingly spirit could not crush;
For Pride in chains than e'er before
   Is stronger, though with conscious blush.

What prowess thine, by all admired!
　That hedged thine adversary in,
And from " Messala's " grasp aspired
　The victor's laurel crown to win.

One moment, friend and confidante,
　If lovely " Iras " seemed to thee,
The next, a heart like adamant
　Was shown by her duplicity.

The blandishments of cunning art
　In Egypt's fairest daughters were,
Beside the love of " Esther's " heart,
　Like charms of wicked sorcerer.

Apollo's self in comeliness,
　Type of thy people Israel!　　　　·
In Roman garb, a Jew no less
　Who loved his land and kindred well.

O champion of thy hapless race!
　Our sympathies were all with thee ·
In thy desire to see His face
　And serve " The King Who Was To Be."

The Fortune-Teller.

" Gypsy, skilled in chiromancy,
　　Telling fortunes by the hand,
Satisfy my longing fancy —
　　Answer all that I demand!

" Dark, mysterious clairvoyant!
　　Is there in my horoscope
Aught to make my spirits buoyant
　　In the promises of hope?

" Whisper, soul of divination,
　　Thou who canst the future see!
Whose the heart in adoration
　　Shall its queen acknowledge me?

" Or if woe, not weal, betide me,
　　And of life's supremest bliss
Sweet experience be denied me,
　　What shall take the place of this?"

Thus a maiden fair and merry,
　　On her cheeks the roses' hue,
Lips the deeper shade of cherry,
　　Did the sybil interview.

" Maiden! palmistry my art is,
　　Leagued am I with powers that be,
Known to me the human heart is —
　　All its guarded mystery.

" But there's something in thy beauty,
　In thy tone so gay and glad,
Makes me recreant to my duty
　As a palmist — I am sad.

" Not always thus hard and wrinkled
　Was the face confronting thine,
And the love-light never twinkled
　Once in brighter eyes than mine.

" Years ago had I a daughter,
　Fair and beautiful as thou ;
How I loved, and loving taught her
　Evil thought to disallow.

" This sweet child was rudely taken,
　Stolen from my side away ;
I a wand'rer now forsaken,
　Seek my darling night and day.

" For her sake no drop of sorrow
　Would I pour on thy young heart ;
By the stars, whose aid I borrow,
　Hope and cheer would I impart.

" In thy slender palm extended,
　Half-afraid my own to touch,
Lines in pink and white are blended
　Intricate, expressing much.

"This betokens fame and glory
  Thou art destined yet to win;
That repeats the 'new old story'
  All thy hopes are centered in.

"This"—with closer clasp she caught her—
  "Aye! that mark I know too well—
Eloise! my long-lost daughter!"
  As she tottered, swooned, and fell.

Wond'ring that such mood befell her,
  Tenderly they raised her head;
But, alas! the fortune-teller—
  She, the gypsy-queen, was dead.

Penelope.

With new delight again we've read
  The story of Penelope—
Her patient weaving of the thread
  Into a fabric, fair to see,
Whose consummation it is said
  Should seal at once her destiny.

Her task was ever just begun;
  For artfulness as promptly spoiled,
As soon as each day's work was done,
  The textile web at which she toiled
From early morn till set of sun—
  And thus her anxious suitors foiled.

O, baffled courtiers! ye who sued
　　A hero's loyal wife to gain!
For untold centuries ye have stood
　　As targets for the world's disdain;
While she, a queen beloved and good,
　　Is honored still in Virtue's reign.

Let modern suppliants profit by
　　The lesson, efficacious still
Though learned, alas! with face awry;
　　That impolitic, imbecile,
And " born to rue " are they who try
　　To circumvent a woman's will.

" Water on the Brain."

'Twas morning; in the Orient
　　The primal rays of daylight shone
Till field and forest's dim extent
　　Took on effulgence, form, and tone;
Anon the mountains' misty sides
　　In far perspective glistened bright
As darkness vanished, that divides
　　As with a curtain day from night.

The thrifty farmer, quick astir
　　At Chanticleer's familiar notes,
Doled out to each dumb servitor
　　His daily share of corn and oats;

And letting down the pasture-bars
　　Advantage gave to lowing kine,
Impatient as untrained hussars
　　To break the ranks of fodder-line.

Then from his ring-streaked, brindled pets,
　　Upon a triple-legged stool
He sat, extracting creamy jets
　　To swell the liquid lactage-pool
Within the pail; and spryly stepped
　　From each to each, and did not bilk
Till all were vacuous — except
　　The cow that gave the buttermilk.

This frothy fluid, looking pure
　　As snowy flakes from Heaven's dome,
By thirsty city epicure
　　Was guzzled in as bovine foam
Excelsior — until one day
　　The cattle, splashing through a bog,
In some unheard-of, wondrous way,
　　Let in the milk a spotted frog

For so the trembling dealer said,
　　Confronted by his customer,
Who bade *him* gulp it down instead
　　Of shamefully deceiving her;
Alas! his produce he might " brook,"
　　But could not brook a woman's scoff —

So with a jerk the can he took
    And tossed its mingled contents off.

Of course *he* never told the tale —
    But enterprising rivals say
Who thrive on his deserted trail:
    " He perished by the ' Milky Way!' "
But, with opinions formed with care,
    Are others who the case explain
In cruel jest — for they declare
    " 'Twas only water on the brain ! "

Too Soon!

A modest violet, azure-eyed,
    Stirred 'neath its dark, protecting mold,
    And whispered, " Why, it can't be cold ! "
To the slumb'ring daisy by its side ;
    " For I am sure I hear the tread
    Of gentle.Spring above my head !

" Her touch is making all things bright —
    For where the snow was wont to drift
    Upon our bed, a widening rift
Lets in the blessed, glad sunlight —
    And I can feel the atmosphere
    So warm, I know that Spring is here !

" I hear a voice that seems to say,
　As from some far-off vernal bower,
　' Come forth, thou earliest Spring flower ! '
It sounds so like the voice of May,
　I think I'll just peep out to see
　If any one is calling me ! "

And so she did — sweet innocent ! —
　Not knowing that above the ground,
　Grim " Old Jack Frost " was prowling round
With footstep light, on mischief bent ;
　And, lo ! — he nipped her from her stem
　While north winds sang her requiem !

" Too soon ! " cried Daisy, in her bed :
　" The early worm is always caught !
　Just see what poor, dear Violet got !
I'll not be quite so fast ! " she said —
　" But I'll appear at a later hour,
　And be the earliest Spring flower."

Sleeping.

A little crib I sat beside,
And watched two stars at eventide
That silken lashes drooped to hide ;
I hummed a song and softly stepped,
And in the dark my vigil kept —
The stars were out — the baby slept !

Tableaux.

The handsome Spanish artist brought
   From his enchanting land by night,
His pictures — a bewitching lot,
   Done all by hand — in pink and white;
An "Indian Girl," a masterpiece —
   We mean a *miss* — terpiece, was placed
On exhibition — with a crease
   Half way between her chin and waist;
At which we marveled, much afraid —
   For he was such a taking chap —
The charming portraiture was made
   While she was sitting on his lap.
Next came the "Japanese," admired
   By all, from lovely top to toe
In shining tinselry attired,
   With eyes cut bias, sleeves to flow;
We took her in until she fell —
   That is, the artist pulled her down —
And then we saw the stunning belle
   Who captivates and sways the town.
When "Expectation" came in play
   As graceful as a waterfall,
We recognized her by the way
   She hung herself upon the wall —
O, dear! what language does convey —
   Of course, she didn't hang herself!

She sat — or stood — the border lay
   With her — inside — upon a shelf;
Can't anybody understand?
   So much explaining takes up time,
And " Time is Money " — and we've planned
   A thousand ways for every dime.
Then later, in that very frame,
   In closest jam — a perfect squeeze,
The " Merry Wives of Windsor " came
   So tight they didn't dare to breathe;
Who was old Windsor, anyhow?
   Like Brigham Young — an awful " Saint "—
With wives the law did not allow,
   Who choked them into meek restraint?
But then they looked so innocent,
   And seemed to like the Mormon plan,
To have and hold, and be content
   With but the fraction of a man;
We saw " Justitia " serene,
   Who on a tub stood upside down —
Oh! why, of course, the tub we mean —
   Now do not criticize and frown!
Had she with honest balance weighed
   Her audience, we do aver
This statuesque, imposing maid
   Had found that all were wanting — her.
The manager, with ready wit
   That never yet was known to fail,

Convulsed us by the happy hit
   Of offering the gems for sale ;
Which made "the pictures" pout and groan,
   When, to avert the war he'd waged,
He said in more emollient tone
   That they were " nearly all engaged."
Old " Castle Garden " showed a scene
   That all who've seen it understand,
For " Jean Crapeau " and " Erin " green
   With " Sauer Kraut?' were hand in hand ;
The " Singing School " wound up the show
   With baton flourish grand and fine,
And when the people rose to go
   The curtain fell on " Auld Lang Syne."

"Holy Land."

Delectable " Holy Land ! " magical book !
In thy pages enchanting, I lingering look,
And oft am transported in rapture, to dwell
In the midst of the scenes thou portrayest so well.

With thee, I have crossed the broad ocean, and seem
To behold every valley and mountain and stream
That burst on thy vision, and thrilled thee with joy,
And a memory left, Time can never destroy.

Historic Old England I've traversed, and stood
Beside sculptured tombs of the great and the good;
And oft, in Earth's corners neglected, have found
Lone graves that must ever be hallowed ground.

The steep Alpine track I have climbed without fear,
While the sound of the avalanche greeted my ear;
And, surmounting those crowns of perpetual snow,
Looked down on the beautiful valley below.

top of St. Peter's magnificent dome
surveyed the vast city of Rome
ling emotions, and tried to recall
and grandeur, her pride and her fall.

ie were streets that once echoed the tread
ring armies — and there captive led,
l, though in fetters rejoicingly trod,
And sealed with his life his devotion to God.

I've been awed by the Sphinx and the Pyramids, while
Ascending the sacred, mysterious Nile,
That still floweth on through green valleys, as when
In Egypt ruled Joseph — a prince among men.

I've wandered where Thebes, of historic renown,
That once of the civilized world was the crown,
In desolate ruins, seems sadly to say,
Earth's grandeur and glory thus yield to decay.

3

But the wish of my heart, my life-dream was fulfilled,
And with sacred emotions my spirit was thrilled,
When my gaze rested first on the valleys so green,
Of that holiest land upon earth — Palestine!

There in sweet meditation I " walked by the sea "
Oft blest by His presence — O, bright Galilee!
And a beautiful picture my memory fills
Of a mirror, encased in a frame-work of hills.

I have climbed to the summit, and cannot forget
The memories that cling around thee, Olivet!
What scenes have occurred in Gethsemane's shade,
Where Jesus hath knelt, and in agony prayed.

I've " walked about Zion," and lingered to see
The spot where Redemption was purchased for me ;
And shared in the deep-thrilling awe that awaits
The stranger who enters Jerusalem's gates.

All the teachings of childhood came over me, when
I followed where He, the dear Saviour of men,
" Went about doing good "— for wherever He trod,
Are recognized still — the foot-prints of God.

O glorious Land! that has witnessed the birth
And the death of our Saviour — no land upon earth
More favored than thou — and till life shall depart
Of thee, blessed memories shall dwell in my heart.

Block Island.

Oh ! billow-chafed and wind-swept isle,
   Engirt by rugged seas ;
Forsaken by the traveler,
Forgotten by the sojourner,
Bereft of beauty's grace and smile
   And summer indices !

An ocean-field with ice afloat
   Thy crystal setting is ;
The shifting floe, for daring feet
That holds but danger and deceit,
Erewhile that rocked the pleasure boat
   And fed the fisheries.

Through many a league of bleakest space,
   The ray that never dies,
From storm-beleagured Pharos' light
On fair Montauk or Watch Hill height,
Of sail and sailors show no trace
   Beneath the wintry skies.

As once the bold, intrepid Kane,
   Hero adventurous,
For weary months environed lay
A prisoner in an Arctic bay,
So thou art bosomed in the main —
   A frigid nautilus.

O lonely isle! the very wave
  That, like a gem impearled,
Shall hold thee sparkling on its breast
In bud and bloom and verdure dressed,
Enfolds thee now as in the grave —
  Cut off from all the world.

The Dear Remaining Few.

The touch beneficent of Spring
  Shall clothe the hill and vale and plain
With verdure, bloom, and everything
  That makes this world a fair domain ;
But none of these can gladness bring
  To our sad hearts, or wake the strain
In other days we used to sing —
  Days that will never come again!

Though rich and beautiful her dower
  As ever graced an earthly throne,
Still desolate the fairest bower   ·
  If we must walk therein alone ;
Or pass a solitary hour
  No friendly hand to clasp our own ;
Can song of bird, or hue of flower
  Make up for one dear face or tone ?

With heavy pinions hovering,
  It seems that Death is in the air,
The whole bright world o'ershadowing;
  For friends are falling everywhere,
To whom, departed, still we cling;
  Life's promises were all so fair,
And in their presence comforting
  We took no note of time or care.

Around the crumbling walls of clay,
  Their home from ours that now divide,
In summer-time shall children play
  And lovers walk at eventide;
While anguish words cannot portray,
  Our hearts must bear, too oft allied
To futile questionings why they,
  In grace and beauty, should have died.

O Angel dread! whose wings have fanned
  The cheeks that bore the roses' hue
With blighting power, whose fateful hand
  Sweet lips has touched, like poison-dew —
Behold! a few yet proudly stand
  Beside us, brave and strong and true!
Though but a remnant of our band,
  O spare the dear remaining few!

3*

A Great Singer.

The tears were dropping softly down
   Upon my polonaise —
A velvet vine-embroidered gown,
   A "Dolly Varden craze" —
When through the door a little maid
   Came with a timid rap,
And looking up in wonder laid
   A pansy in my lap.

"Don't cry!" she said, and turned away,
   And I saw her not for years,
Whose presence like a sunbeam lay
   Across the path of tears;
Till in a Western town one night
   Amid a rapturous throng
I sat beneath the calcium light,
   To greet the queen of song.

The debutante, that gifted child,
   Had been beyond the sea,
And learned to trill the linnet's wild,
   Sweet notes of melody;
Had caught the prima donna's role,
   Marchesi's pupil apt,
And caroled till her tuneful soul
   Grow tremulous and rapt.

Not Jenny Lind nor Malibran
  Sang more divinely sweet,
Or held, as only divas can,
  Adorers at their feet;
That heavenly maid Calliope,
  Among her worshipers,
Had been distraught with jealousy
  To hear a voice like hers.

But while the world in homage bowed
  To recognize her gift,
I only saw a sable cloud
  Through which a golden rift
Of sunlight cleared the mists away;
  And standing in the gap
Was she who laid, on that sad day,
  A pansy in my lap.

O cantatrice! sing for aye,
  And still be good and kind
As when with childish naïveté
  My sorrow you divined;
And for your Fame-crowned womanhood,
  While dear affection swells
With thoughts of " Auld Lang Syne " renewed,
  Accept Love's immortelles.

Smoke.

'Twas a zero morn, and the air was keen
As a glittering blade of Damascene,
And gathering frost on the window told
An icy tale of the piercing cold;
From savory viands that formed the base
Of the matin meal — and a whispered grace —
I watched the vapors curling away
From a thousand flues in the morning gray,
And thus to my jubilant *vis-a-vis*,
Who like a comet eclipses me,
With sudden thought impetuous spoke:
" Why, what becomes of the clouds of smoke ?"

Do they center and form those misty piles
That drink in light like beautiful isles
On the boundless face of the sea of sky ?
Or low on Orion, like shadows nigh,
Untold anathemas bringing down
For tingeing astral castles brown,
Do they tell star-dwellers what earth must be
By its dense, exhalant impurity ?
That light and grace and bloom we lack,
Our globe is drear and our skies are black,
Earth's denizens never bereft of a tear
Because of the poisonous atmosphere ?

Or away on some old plantation ground
Where freedmen's cabins cluster round,
And Dinah's bit of tinder stuff
Emits one feeble, flickering puff,
Do fumes of Northern wood and coal
With Southern exhalations roll,
And like the clasp of friendly hands
Above those reunited lands
In mingled waves suffuse the air —
And, like the blessing after prayer,
Descend on grass-grown battle plains
In winter snows or summer rains?

Do they circle away in vanishing lines
To rest on the tops of soughing pines
In the wilderness where the moose-deer roams
As wild as Zulus in Afric' homes;
Where anglers revel encamped about
The limpid haunts of the speckled trout,
Where the lumber-camp and woodman's axe
Efface the wild opossum's tracks;
Where Androscoggin's waters sweep
A mighty pathway to the deep,
And honest Dow and Statesman Blaine
Adorn like stars the brow of Maine?

Or are they wafted, soon or late,
To El Dorado's "Golden Gate,"

And tossed about by every gale
That rends Pacific's stoutest sail,
But redwood giants move no more
Than Zephyr's breath the iron door?
Perchance like nebulæ awhile
They hang o'er Santa Barbara's isle;
Precursor of discomfort hid
In the weary heart of the invalid,
To whom the months' incessant rain
And sunshine's loss is added pain.

O wandering vapors! like the breeze
That rocks the navies of the seas —
To intermix with London fog
The city's arteries to clog,
Or dimly veil the face serene
Of proud Britannia's sovereign queen —
Though North or South, or West or East
Diffusing like the foamy yeast,
O errant vapors! lost in space
Like shreds of fine illusion lace,
To other worlds bear not the joke
That *ours* is wreathed in tobacco-smoke!

Worry.

Contentment reigning in the heart
    Knows never fuss nor flurry;
It is not work that wears one out
    But everlasting worry.

If Others Would.

If other human beings had
  The goodness that is his,
The tender love and sympathy,
  The winning courtesies,
This world would never be the vale
  Of sorrow that it is.

If other mortals would extend
  A helping hand to those
Who, by untoward Fate, endure
  Misfortune's cruel blows,
Prosperity and happiness
  Would blossom as the rose.

If others would but learn of him,
  In hearts of gratitude
Who must forever be enshrined —
  O, if they only would,
Each in his own appointed place
  Might do a world of good!

No preacher nor philosopher,
  Nor saintly acolyte,
More clearly understands that Earth
  Cannot be Eden quite —
And yet he bears a cheerful part
  In setting it aright.

Tuberoses.

O rarest of flowers! that seem to exhale
On the stillness of air, or the breath of the gale,
All effluent odors in botany shrined;
The volatile essences richly combined
Of orchis diffusions, deliciously blent
With lavender, orange, and balsamine scent.

No jessamine chalice or hyacinth vase,
No mignonette-perfumed or blossoming space
Of violets redolent, dewy and sweet,
With delicate fragrance is half so replete,
As one of these exquisite florets that hold
The cream of aroma in waxen-like mold.

There's a "Flowery Kingdom" way over the sea,
The home of the Mongol, the "heathen Chinee"—
But *why* this cognomen of fanciful sound
Applies to their bit of terrestrial ground,
No pundit can tell, be he ever so wise,
And chance if Confucius himself could surmise.

But Yankees, quick-witted and willing to guess,
Are equally ready and free to confess —
By "coolies" imported who slavishly toil
As cheap as the dirt on American soil —
That every known spot where a Chinaman dwells
Is held in remembrance — because of its "smells."

And so, to preserve our dear continent free
From Eastern effluvium, what can there be
More potent and lasting in counter-effect,
The dainty olfactory sense to protect,
Than lovely tuberoses, ambrosial and rare,
In fine distillations suffusing the air?

And as in the ocean when refuse is tossed,
By free salination impurity's lost,
So these liliaceous corolla-cups bear
In happier living a recognized share;
And prove their beneficence, beauty, and worth
Refining, adorning, and sweetening earth.

Destruction of Flood Rock.

O restless man! unsatisfied
    With Earth whence sprung thy parent-tree,
Upon whose branches far and wide
    Hang jewels of thy pedigree,
Fair scions touched with family pride
    That marks their true heredity!

Doth not this mundane planet, graced
    With light and bloom and beauty sweet,
By its Designer firmly placed
    Beneath thy own inconstant feet,
Respond to thy fastidious taste,
    Or its requirements kindly meet?

4

The cascade leaping from its source,
   A crystal spring upon the hill,
Becomes a mighty water-course
   Subservient to thy slightest will,
And gives of its unfailing force   ·
   To guide the loom or turn the mill.

The monarchs of the forest bow
   Beneath the sturdy woodman's axe,
The glebe unrolls before the plow
   A furrow for the yeoman's tracks,
And science from the mountain-brow
   Discerns a planet's parallax.

The billowy sea, that danced and laughed
   And man's dominion long defied,
Bears on its bosom princely craft —
   Palatial ships that proudly glide;
Or flying sail that breezes waft
   With speed that rivals time and tide.

Yet combating alike rebuff
   Or ridicule, unlimited
Is man's ambition — not enough
   The scope of his victorious tread
Till ocean-reefs, sea-chafed and rough,
   Are riven in their stony bed.

A little hand so soft and white
   Impels the swift electric spark,
The hidden fuse that shall ignite
   In submarine recesses dark,
Which like a flash of Heaven's light
   Goes straight to its projected mark.

As if the dreaded Typhoon gale
   Had vexed the spirit of the main,
Uprose an instantaneous wail
   Of subterranean rage and pain ;
As when that ancient temple-vail
   By power divine was rent in twain.

As if Titanic power lay
   In youth's dexterity and grace,
Or as a giant would convey
   Neptunian rocks through airy space,
So scattered fragments leagues away
   Of sunken ledges wrenched apace.

Rejoice, O mariner ! to thee
   Shall " Hell-Gate " nevermore present
An obstacle that may not be
   By man's devices circumvent,
Till hither vessels ride as free
   As Arab from his desert-tent.

As calm succeds the tempest's roar,
  So elements are reconciled ;
Now, conqueror of sea and shore,
  Since " Peace on Earth " again hath smiled,
Be thou contented evermore
  And led — as by a little child !

Inauguration Day, 1887.

Ascending smoke from countless flues,
  Like floating nebulæ,
Hung over snowy avenues
  As trackless as the sea ;
Where rural lane and city street
  Unbroken stretches lay,
Beneath the sun that rose to greet
  Inauguration Day.

Inspirited by fife and drum,
  Militia bands enrolled.
From office, bench, and counter come
  Like minute-men of old ;
A glittering retinue, who led
  The chosen ruler's way
With serried ranks and martial tread,
  Inauguration Day.

Not fairer was that world renowned,
    Suburb Pantheon dome,
That like a storied temple crowned
    Antique and classic Rome,
Than Hartford's stately edifice,
    In festival array
Like some enthroned impératrice,
    Inauguration Day.

Proud Capitol! in chiseled grace
    Like beauty's sculptured queen,
Environing in council space
    A grand impressive scene,
That angels must have thrilled to see;
    Who registered for aye
Those solemn vows of fealty,
    Inauguration Day.

As governors thus come and go,
    May each unsullied be
And wear like garments of the snow
    The robe of purity;
In fair Connecticut— our State —
    May rectitude hold sway,
And love of justice consecrate
    Inauguration Day.

4*

"Old Folks."

Mysteries of election day
Yet had scarcely cleared away,
Ere attention all was drawn
To a strange phenomenon —
Wondrous transformation rare
Happening at our fancy "Fair."

In the twinkling of an eye —
Not a shade of reason why —
Rosy maidens, laughing-eyed,
Ruddy youth, our hope and pride,
All their bloom and freshness lost —
Like carnations nipped by frost.

Heads as suddenly grew white
As if due to awful fright,
While the sobriquet "Antiques"
Rose from costume's crazy freaks;
For such robes, put on at dark,
Might have come from "Noah's ark."

Spirit full of revelry,
First appeared in ecstasy
She whose ruff and spacious dress
Marked the days of good "Queen Bess" —
While our modern queen took on
Style of "Martha Washington."

"George " was hanging round near by —
He who could not " tell a lie " —
When the " flour-pot," he said,
" Had been emptied on his head,"
We believed him, — for we knew —
By his locks — it must be true !

Charmed by " Jacob's " fluent tongue,
To his arm, confiding, clung
" Rachel " — saucy, sweet, and quaint —
Far from being solemn saint!
Even in grandmother's cap,
Still admired by many a chap !

Could it be that " fourteen years' "
Alternating hopes and fears,
Waiting for his " Rachel " fair,
Thus had bleached out " Jacob's " hair —
Carved his alabaster skin,
Put those extra wrinkles in ?

Clad in antiquated rig,
Snowy cue and periwig,
Polished, graceful, well at ease,
Prodigal in arts to please, —
Who'd have thought that courtly man
Was " our bashful, modest Dan ? "

Thus, in highest style of art,
Each so well assumed his part

In fantastic, odd disguise,
That we scarce could recognize
One of that capricious set
Whom an hour before we met.

Sweet delusion! born to last
Only till the " Fair " had passed!
For with morn's succeeding dawn
Every trace of age was gone;
While the " box receipt " supply
" Our piano " helped to buy.

My Art.

As if my unpretending rhymes
　Publicity might ever claim,
Or echo rapture as in chimes
　Resounding from the bells of Fame!
I never dreamed of such renown,
　And only wrote because my heart
Provoked the same resistless frown
　Whene'er I tried to fetter art.

The solemn grandeur of the sea,
　The beauty of the summer sky,
The song-bird's revel, wild and free,
　In rhythm spake to ear and eye,
Till melody possessed my soul;

And Poesy, as if astir
The measured numbers to control,
Became its meet interpreter.

And other hearts that throbbed as mine,
Intensified and thrilled no less,
Grew covetous of every line
So facile-traced that could express
Their undivulged, unuttered thought;
And praised each lyric pseudo gem,
And gratefully the singer sought
In metric strains who sang for them.

I have not borrowed of the books
That teach symmetric, polished phrase,
Nor delved in musty, classic nooks;
Nor dared to penetrate the maze
Of Concord's deep philosophy —
And Buddhist fallacies I hate;
For never shall *my* Heaven be
An aimless, vague, Nirvana-state.

But narrow-sphered to critic sight,
Have I with true, unsullied pen
In kindliness essayed to write
As one who loves his fellow-men;
And when my gift persisted in
Hath wakened some accordant note,
It hath to me sweet solace been
And Sorrow's potent antidote.

As use and polish render bright
    The rusty cimeter of steel,
So poor endowments turned aright
    An unsuspected grace reveal;
And thus I dream, and feel, and know
    That in celestial atmosphere,
To full fruition yet shall grow
    The bud of talent lent me here.

Amid the Corn.

When roasting ears are peeping through
    Their silken tassel curls,
When corn leaves glisten in the dew
    Like ribbons strewn with pearls;
When Phœbus' splendor is revealed
    And gilds the summer morn,
I love to walk the furrowed field
    Among the rows of corn.

It brings to mind those vanished days
    In adolescence sweet,
When through familiar seas of maze
    With ardent, childish feet
That never tired, the glebe I trod
    The " hired man " to warn
Where grew the tares, or where a clod
    Obstructed hills of corn.

A happy home upon the farm
  In memory holds a place,
That city life with all its charm
  Can never quite efface.
O give me back the days of yore!
  When I, a farmer born,
In pantalet and pinafore
  Grew up amid the corn.

O that I could to nature true
  From etiquette relax,
And follow, as I used to do,
  Papa's unerring tracks!
A scholar, who could wield the pen,
  Whose honors well were borne,
Was he — this noblest, best of men —
  Who plowed and hoed the corn.

I'd rather be, though dumb and droll,
  An effigy to-day,
A man of straw upon a pole
  To scare the crows away,
Than like a figure fashion-spun
  A palace to adorn,
Disdainfully look down on one
  Who works amid the corn.

The Difference.

Love is no restricted part
Of a woman's trusting heart,
Balancing in like degrees
Other traits and qualities,
Like a " corner lot" of bliss
In its guarded edifice ;
'Tis her very life wrapped up
In the secret treasure cup
Of her soul — its vital sense
Holding proud pre-eminence
Over every other thought;
'Tis a ray supernal caught
From effulgence round the Throne —
" God is Love" — and He alone.

Love in man is little more
Than a ripple passing o'er
The deep current of a life
With untold diversions rife ;
Either knotty points of law
All his aspirations draw,
Or resistless struggles he
With some new theology ;
Or, as children play with blocks,
Notes the rise and fall of stocks,

Fraternizes " bulls and bears,"
Speculating unawares
Till his soul in not a cleft
Hath for love a " margin " left.

Maiden with the blooming cheek,
But a word to thee we speak ;
If a man shall say : " To you,
O, my love ! my heart is true
As the needle to the pole —
Day-star art thou of my soul !
If thou look disdainfully
On my suit, repelling me,
All the solace that I crave
Shall be this — an early grave —
And the finale to thy scoff,
My untimely taking off ! "
Do not on his words rely —
Just for love men never die !

But, creation's lord, if thou
Cherishest a mutual vow,
Do not, we admonish thee,
Let the monster jealousy
Drive thy sweetheart to despair ;
Tempting her to say : " Beware,
Faithless one ! do not forget
Love shall be requited yet ;

Glistening on yonder green
Shall a double cross be seen ;
Since thy perfidy I've known
I will die — but not alone ! ''
O believe her — sure as fate
She will do it — soon or late !

At Sea.

The victim of miscarried plans,
   This rueful self, as all may see,
   A pouting " ward in chancery,"
Perforce abideth yet on lands
As hot as arid desert-sands ;
   But that immortal spirit-part,
   Mine *alter ego*, longing heart,
     Whatever it may be,
     Is far away at sea.

Like unspent geysers pours the heat,
   O'erflows its crucible of brass,
   Makes crispy sward of verdant grass,
To lava-beds converts the street,
And sears the soles of tender feet ;
   While dear copartners wonder much
   If this intense caloric touch
     Affects my fancies free —
     O never ! I'm at sea !

What though the torrid atmosphere
   This " too, too solid flesh " transform
   Into a compound soft and warm,
And sad companions drop a tear
O'er one who lies unburied here!
   It is not I — I'm on the wave —
   In cool circumfluence I lave
     And pure felicity,
     A nereid of the sea.

Seek I a kingdom? 'tis the main!
   Where I may smile at billows high,
   The vortex of the deep defy,
Consort with him whose potent reign
Encompasses the watery plain ;
   Or with admiring, ardent eyes
   Behold the glorious sunset skies,
     In rainbow mystery,
     That beautify the sea.

Mais il est mal à propos though,
   That some resistless, secret art
   Hath forced the spirit to depart;
For everywhere I chance to go,
That is — this empty shell — I know
   That friends who value my caress
   Remark my absent-mindedness,
     And wish the soul of me
     Were not so far — at sea.

𝔑𝔬𝔱 𝔐𝔦𝔫𝔢 𝔄𝔩𝔬𝔫𝔢.

The landscape, that in verdure glows
With all the freshness of the rose,
In myriad forms of beauty, throws
   A spell of rapture o'er me;
As like a queen upon her throne,
From lofty parapet alone
I view, admire, and call my own
   The hills and vales before me.

Yes; all is mine, of beauty wrought
By superhuman skill and thought—
A priceless heritage, which naught
   Can wrest from my possession
While satellites in splendor shine,
And joyous sounds, and prospects fine,
On every thrilling sense combine
   To make their true impression.

In rare, pellucid atmosphere,
Through tangled boughs afar I peer —
Receptacles of hidden cheer
   In fruitage, ripe and ruddy;
Like odd designs in arabesque,
Though wild, fantastic, and grotesque,
Presenting scenes so picturesque
   I fain would pause to study.

In parting benison benign
The sunset glow, like mellow wine,
Irradiates this wealth of mine
   With marvelous refulgence;
Like that a mortal blest perceives
On " one of those ambrosial eves
A day of storms so often leaves,"
   To crown its wild indulgence.

The aureole, o'er field and town,
Might tempt a wandering seraph down
To view that iridescent crown
   Whose brilliance so enchants me.
I can but wonder if it be
The splendor of reality,
Through some supernal agency,
   Or due to necromancy.

All beauty, charm, and novelty
Beneath the sky, is not for me
Alone the heritage; for he
   Who hath an ear to hear it,
Or eye to see — it matters not —
With true esthetic ardor fraught,
May claim whatever God hath wrought
   For eye, and ear, and spirit.

And who, with highest sense endued,
From boundless riches, oft renewed,

Would choose the best of all that's good,
    Will find his chief employment
In lonely haunt, or busy mart,
In searching out that valued part;
To treasure it within his heart,
    A well-spring of enjoyment.

On Reading Swinburne.

Poet! thou hast wondrous art,
    Rare as necromantic skill!
Thou canst touch the coldest heart,
Life and love to it impart,
Make the crystal tear-drop start
As, unchained, thy fancies dart
    Hither, thither, at thy will.

Words but playthings are to thee —
    Which like happy child among
Thou dost revel fearless, free,
Leaping oft the boundary
Of conventionality,
By the strength of imagery
    In thy metric mother-tongue.

Taken at thy very best,
    There's a " lilt in every line "
That, in rude plebeian breast,

Might awaken deep unrest;
Fire the blood of one possessed
Even of a royal crest,
   Scion of a kingly line.

Thine is matchless eloquence —
   Thou a benefactor born!
As, endowed with prescience,
Thou dost search out vain pretense
'Neath the garb of innocence,
And in true benevolence
   Hold it up to human scorn.

Does that winged steed Pegasus —
   He who threw Bellerophon —
Risky as a blunderbuss,
Frisking round so mischievous,
Ever show his animus
Mettlesome, and hazardous
   To thy safety, Algernon?

As enchanted we peruse
   Stanzas rich in polished lore,
Envy we the power that woos,
In Parnassian interviews
With thy generous patron muse,
Favors none knew how to use
   Half so gracefully before.

Who so prodigal to thee?
  King of meters, tell us, do!
Is it fair Calliope —
Goddess eloquent is she —
Or divine Melpomene?
Tell thy secret, so may we
  Importune the muses, too!

For, O Swinburne! to thy height
  We — poor publican afar —
Downcast and despairing quite,
Dare not lift our eyes, but smite
On our bosom day and night;
Thou the sun in splendor bright —
  We, not even a tiny star!

"Young Society-Darwin."

In vestments fine, the latest plan,
The tailor had arrayed him;
  His low-necked jacket, light rattan,
And staring lens betrayed him;
  But in our hearts we never can
Find language to upbraid him,
  But try to call this thing — a man!
Because the Lord hath made him.

En Hiver.

Le long de la rue neigeuse,
Dans la saison rigoureuse,
   Je passe souvent,
Tout oubliant la tempête
Qui frappe autour de ma tête
   Furieusement.

Sans peur, sans souci, sans peine,
Je marche comme une reine,
   Essayant avoir
L'air bon ; rencontrant l'orage
À bras ouverts, mon visage
   Éclatant d'espoir.

Sous son tapis blanc la terre,
Une grande mer de verre,
   Quand vient le printemps
Fleurira comme la rose ;
Nous donnant beaucoup de cause
   Pour contentement.

Parmi la neige à l'aurore,
Ou en regardant la flore,
   Je me satisfais ;
Car l'étoile d'espérance
Peint le ciel de l'existence
   Le teint violet.

Evolution.

Ho, everybody! an hour purloin
　From time's brief distribution
Of leisure moments, just to join
　The " class in evolution."

To all the world tuition's free —
　A school with no defection,
No begging for admission-fee,
　And better, no collection.

Did love for geologic laws,
　The all-prevailing passion,
Lead us?　Oh, no!　we went because
　To go was all the fashion.

For we had loved to stare at stars
　On some ambrosial even;
Or, through the moonlight's argent bars,
　Look longingly to Heaven.

Or, far removed from haunts of men,
　This mundane sphere forgetting,
Admire that distant sky-land when
　The golden sun was setting.

Then, presto! what a fall was there!
　As landed 'mid the strata
Of subterranean regions, where
　The darkness dims the data.

In eloquent, unwritten speech,
   Defying skill of sages,
To read what rocks so grandly teach
   About the vanished ages.

How wonderful ! that science can
   Bridge o'er the mighty chasm
Between the dear, developed man
   And shapeless bioplasm.

Yet, every mite that ever groped
   Before or after Noah
Is classified and microscoped,
   And labelled " Protozoa."

By evolution laws we find,
   Though dimly comprehended,
That vertebrates of human kind
   Are from a worm descended.

Again 'tis said — does logic fall ? —
   Because we've heard a dozen
Times, at least, that every whale
   Is our primeval cousin.

Propounding theories like these
   Nobody seems to bother ;
And we may choose whate'er we please
   For our revered forefather.

Imagination runs away —
  For what is there to hinder,
When all the wise logicians say
  That water is a cinder?

In his most lucid interval
  Did anybody think it —
That aqua, too, is a mineral?
  And so, how dare we drink it?

So marvelous and plausible
  Are these advanced ideas
Unto a world already full
  Of ills — and panaceas,

And all explained in tones as clear
  As softly tinkling cymbal;
Not sounding brass beguiles the ear,
  But cultured Mr. Kimball.

But, touching our ancestral tree,
  Our filial doting spirit
Resents the thought, and sighs that we
  Were ever born to hear it.

By turns we scowl and smile and grieve,
  Then grow severely spunky;
Because we *never will* believe
  That man — was once a *monkey!*

His Potent Pen.

A power was his unique and strange,
  That held the world entranced ;
Beyond whose utmost, loftiest range,
  By easy flights advanced,
He soared, and wrought amid the stars
The diction that no blemish mars.

He touched his pen and moved so free —
  Because he willed it so —
The waves of Thought's tremendous sea :
  Whose ever-widening flow
Still circled in controlling reach
Of purpose marked by polished speech.

What was it lay in a bit of steel,
  A nib of gold, or quill,
That made the world accordant feel
  As touched with tender thrill ?
Why, only this — his potent pen
Was dipped in love for his fellow-men !

How She Went Away.

We bade her good-night, looking into her eyes
Already that shone with celestial surprise,
And when we returned — a brief interval-space —
A beautiful angel had taken her place.

"Old Liberty Bell."

O, Liberty herald! thy echoes I hear,
As down through the century, year after year,
The resonant voice that our forefathers knew,
Triumphant and thrilling, still loyal and true,
In pæans rings out o'er the land that we love,
Proclaiming good-will to the people thereof.

In thy reverberations sonorously mix
With the patriot spirit of Seventy-Six,
The soul, that seems wafted from some distant shore
As if intervening, rough seas passing o'er,
Of " Old Independence," obedience to God,
Resistance to tyrants at home and abroad.

From the bosom of Earth wast thou, Liberty Bell,
In crude metal taken, and fashioned so well,
And by skillful artificer given a tongue
In the City of Brotherly Love that first rung,
As Victory's bright, starry pennon unfurled
To the uplifted gaze of a wondering world.

Old Liberty Bell! though corroded with rust,
And choked and half-buried 'neath undisturbed dust,
And haplessly cracked on that memorable day
In overstrained efforts to greet Henry Clay,
Thy clarion notes of the past resound yet,
Recalling the days we would never forget.

Now, Liberty Bell, on thy way to the South,
Thy history travels before; every mouth
Can the story repeat of the stirring events
That led to the birth-day of Freedom — and hence
To our proud elevation, and paramount worth —
Admired and honored all over the Earth.

May favors auspicious thy wand'rings attend,
And greetings fraternal from Northern hearts blend
With those of our neighbors, till courtesies kind
Shall "many in one" so harmoniously bind,
That in jubilant tones shall thy aged tongue tell
Of a country united, O Liberty Bell!

The Reason Why.

The bobolink and oriole
    Are wild with blithesome singing;
Each pouring out his happy soul
In gleeful notes beyond control,
    Till melody is ringing
In forest, field, and orchard gay
With countless blossoms' rich array.

The pendant leaf is never still,
    The bending twigs are dancing
As if in rapt, accordant thrill

With every fresh, spontaneous trill
　From tuneful throats, enhancing
The gladness and the glory of
Sweet May, the month that warblers love.

Hilarious lad and romping lass,
　Alert in vigor bounding,
Come unawares in meadow grass
On many an interwoven mass
　Of fibers fine, surrounding
That little world where bird and mate
In hope exultant watch and wait.

Thus every nest, half-hidden by
　The verdure round it growing,
A home reveals — explaining why
So gaily sing and lightly fly
　The feathered songsters ; knowing
That in their promised fledgeling brood
Shall song and rapture be renewed.

So, like the birds, the heart doth sing
　In dulcet tone and meter,
That hath some fond, endearing thing
'Round which its tendrils twine and cling ;
　So is existence sweeter
To one who holds in cherished thought
Some love-encircled, home-like spot.

Choosing a Pastor.

Now this is what the deacon said:
(May blessings crown each saintly head!)

" For leagues around we've sought to find
    Some one to fill the place
Who shall our hearts together bind;
An honest man as God designed,
With earnest purpose, cultured mind,
    And liberal share of grace."

Then anxious parents had their say:
(Whose scions claim the right of way!)

" Before the winning flag unfurls
    We clamor for the youth;
'Mid business cares, in social whirls
We cannot train our boys and girls —
Before them, *he* must scatter pearls
    Of wisdom and of truth!"

The young men exercised their brains:
(And for a while forgot their canes!)

" We want a man about our size,
    A manly, whole-souled, genial chap,

II—6*

Who, though he may have won the prize
In Greek and Hebrew exercise,
Can catch a base-ball as it flies,
     Or wear the umpire's cap!"

The lovely maidens shook their curls
And said:—(Oh, my! what saucy girls!)

"Now we won't have a pastor prim
     Or grave, with carping tongue!
He must be handsome, tall, and slim,
Our cavalier in twilight dim,
And we'll lay down our lives for him—
     Of course, he must be young!"

The populace at large chimed in:
(Who dodge the missiles aimed at sin!)

"He may be prophet, king, or priest,
     A 'Tabernacle Saint'
Who has his congregation fleeced,
For aught we care—but this at least
We want—an intellectual feast
     Without sectarian taint!"

Thus everybody aired his views
     About the kind of man

Our wealthy, cultured church should choose
To wear our " Reverend Idol's " shoes ;
But no one dreamed he might refuse
    To come, and spoil our plan.

In course of time we half agreed
    A certain man might do,
Who seemed to apprehend our need ;
But, though particular indeed,
It never entered in " our creed "
    That he might be so, too.

And so, at last, we gave a call
    To him that, to our mind,
Appeared embodiment of all
That we had hoped for — pretty, tall,
Whose many virtues might appall
The careless world in evil thrall ;
In eloquence, bereft of drawl ;
As copious as a waterfall,
Whose bump of avarice was small,
Whom we believed adept at ball ;
    And he — why, he — declined !

Remember the Poor.

·A far greater blessing to us 't will insure,
And a mansion in Heaven will help to secure,
If we have in kindness remembered the poor.

The Ice Palace.

In crystalline splendor a sight to behold,
It rose like Jerusalem's temple of old;
   No sound of a hammer was there,
But block upon block, from the ice-harvest cold
Dissevered and chiseled in exquisite mold,
   Made up its proportions so fair.

Within its broad galleries gracefully wrought,
As solid expressions of fanciful thought,
   A million of luminous beams
More brilliant than stellar rays lighted the spot
That shone like a mermaid's sub-aqueous grot,
   Or the wonderful fabric of dreams.

No cavern stalactic down under the ground,
With drops of bi-carbonate oozing around
   In pensile, calcareous cones ;
No ice-impearled castle has ever been found
With iridal colors so gorgeously crowned
   As this — of prismatical stones.

As if all the rainbows that ever the sun
Had kissed into being were blended in one,
   An arcade of frostwork and dews;
So gleamed in transparency filaments spun
By embryo artists — as chromos begun
   Abounding in scintillant hues.

Not like the renowned Coliseum of Rome,
A structure upreared from foundation to dome
   By men who wore Slavery's gyves;
But Liberty's sons, as if building a home,
Toiled day after day — as with honey and comb
   Do busy bees labor in hives.

A city-full poured through its glistening halls,
Its gelid, pellucid, and argentine walls
   Where traffickers offered their wares;
Tobogganers awkward in blankets and shawls
Who struggled as if with Niagara Falls
   Ascending the slippery stairs.

With flambeau, and rocket, and oriflamme bright,
The Fire King leading his cohorts by night,
   In uniform scarlet and gold,
Besieged the Ice Monarch who ordered aright,
And routed with snow-balls the enemy's light
   And left them in darkness and cold.

The King of the carnival pompously grown
From homage to him so obsequious shown,
   Like Xerxes reviewing his fleet,
In royal habiliments sat on his throne
And issued commands in imperious tone
   To vassalry bowed at his feet.

The festival Queen in bewitching array,
As fair as a maid of Circassia to-day,

With cheeks like twin roses aglow,
Environed by courtiers and satellites gay
Regina, the favorite, tempered her sway
　　As Helios softens the snow.

* 　* 　* 　* 　* 　* 　* 　*

The fête had gone by — but the sovereign pair,
Who gave to the scene a nobility air,
　　As icicles lovingly cling
To the roof of a mansion, in happy despair
Had frozen together and fast to the chair —
Borealis and bride! who will have to stay there
　　Till palaces melt in the spring.

The Sea.

O it was luxury to feel
　　The vital force renewed,
Upon the Crescent strand to kneel
　　In silent gratitude,
And drink the ocean-breezes in
Like cordial balm or medicine!

Rejuvenescence in the air,
　　As borne on pinions fleet,
Betrayed its touch in faces fair
　　And quick, elastic feet,
And bounding pulse of all in quest
Of comfort, happiness, and rest.

What mystery is like the sea?
　Enhancing Life's brief length
By added years' sweet guarantee,
　Recruiting health and strength;
And yet the yawning sepulcher
For many a happy voyager.

Is it some sad, remorseful throb
　Provokes its wild unrest,
That thousands it has dared to rob
　Of whom they loved the best,
And thus — O, irony of Fate!
Bereaved ones seeks to compensate?

As well might we essay to solve
　The riddle of the Sphinx,
As from Oceanus evolve
　That chain of mystic links
That fetters in obscurity
The dark enigma of the sea.

How strange! its benefits to crave
　With ardent impetus,
Or choose rencounter with the wave,
　So often treacherous,
That holds in its profound abyss
A vast, marine necropolis.

The Granger.

Look not upon him with disdain,
  Ye dwellers in the town;
Nor wax facetious as ye mark
  His homespun garb of brown.

"Only a Granger," say the rich,
  The favored upper ten;
And Madame Grundy shuts her doors
  On Nature's noblemen.

"Only a Granger," scoffing cry
  The Wall street bulls and bears,
Who deal in futures, puts, and calls,
  Gambling in watered shares,

And scorn the honest son of toil,
  Who fills a *useful* place;
Who grows, but does not corner, wheat,
  Nor grinds the poor man's face.

"Only a Gwanjah," lisp the dudes,
  Those beings minus brains;
Their habitat, convivial clubs,
  Their food, the heads of canes.

"*Only* a Granger," do you say?
  Aye, but his labor gains
The daily bread of myriads,
  And all mankind sustains.

The city's countless denizens,
    The lowly and the great,
On him depend ; his toil supports
    The fabric of the state.

All honor to the upright men
    Who till our acres broad ;
By tens of thousands they marched forth
    For country, right, and God,

When dark Secession raised her torch,
    With parricidal hand,
To light the fires of civil strife
    In our erst-happy land.

And country-nurtured statesmen oft
    In halls of Congress sit,
Who yield to none in intellect,
    Ability, or wit.

While dudes adjust their single lens,
    Or puff the " Cameo,"
The farmer ponders the nation's weal,
    E'en as he plies the hoe.

Ye dandies, reverence this man,
    In coat of faded hue ;
Ye are not worthy to unloose
    His dusty cowhide shoe.

O lady-killer exquisite,
 With face devoid of tan,
Go, swing the scythe and drive the plow,
 And learn to be a *man*.

HARRY HOWARD.

Somnium Poetae.

Omnia nunc nix arva tegit, premit alba viasque,
Frigidaque glacies ramis dependet ab altis
Arborum, et in fluviis vitrea sub veste teguntur
Undique nunc latices, et hiems superat mala terram.
Sed mihi jam veris signa adparent venientis;
Collibus ecce caput se evolvens tollit ad auras
Flos violae, dulcis melioris nuntius horae.
Tum laetus tam dulce poeta patore fenestrae
Spectans, somnit agros segetum messi locupletes;
Junix candida arat, pellit genialis arator;
Querci sub patera recubans umbra, ipse tuetur,
Cum volucres cantant, et formosissima Tellus.
Atque procul pastor pecus amplum ducit in arvis,
Errando atque canit modulamina rustica avena.
Et — sed nunc subito glaciei moles cadit alto
Ab tecto, factusque fragor, monet atque poetam
Jam esse hiemem, nondumque aestatis tempus adesse;
Evigilat, piget et vatem, versatque fenestra.

HARRY HOWARD.

"Sugaring Off."

Round after round in rugged tramp,
　But wholesome discipline,
By sturdy hands about the camp
　The sap was gathered in ;
When one .perspiring, very red,
　And sitting on a trough,
"To close the season," so he said,
　Proposed to "sugar off."

Beyond the farm-house still and white,
　Beyond the poplar bars,
A lignous pile emitted light
　That paled the brighest stars ;
Where caldrons hung, like those of which
　The Bard of Avon told,
With ebullition contents rich
　Above the flame of gold.

A score or more of beaux and belles
　On toothsomeness intent,
Like buzzing bees in flower-dells
　Inhaled the maple scent ;
Who danced around in impish glee
　Like witches in Macbeth,
And stirred the sweet consistency,
　And laughed till out of breath.

In fidget spells, by trial sips
　　Of liquid boiling hot,
How many burned their saucy lips;
　　And pouted at the thought
Of strips of plaster stretched across
　　Each rosy orifice,
Or sighed in secret o'er the loss
　　Of some prospective kiss.

Anon, the mass like melted wax
　　Electrified their hopes,
Who followed out diversion's tracks
　　By making candy ropes;
That by mysterous lasso twirls —
　　How, record never tells —
Glued ribbon-bows and spiral curls
　　To overcoat lapels.

How many lads in languid pose
　　Leaned later 'gainst the trees,
The sticky syrup on their clothes,
　　The 'lasses on their knees —
That is, the sugar! — never yet
　　Hath language run so fast —
But one can never quite forget
　　What happened decades past.

Such fun beyond the curfew hour
　　A Puritan might rue,

Or like an unbelieving Giaour
 Deny the statement true;
But so it was — till *Pater* (and
 A lantern) caused surprise,
Who quite broke up the festive band
 And captured their supplies.

O, with a wild remembrance-thrill
 My heart in rapture beats!
The egg-shell cups again I fill
 With granulated sweets,
And mold in scalloped patty-pans
 Delicious maple cakes
As yellow as the golden sands,
 But pure as snowy flakes.

I've been, as by the drift of chance,
 A wanderer for years
From those delightful, happy haunts
 That memory endears;
But never life hath been so bright
 As when, upon a trough
With Peter Stump, one blessed night
 I helped to " sugar off."
  * * * * *

And for *his* sake, where'er he is,
 This rustic ode I pen
To stir his risibilities;
 The jolliest of men,

7*

Though Prelate of the Holy See;
   Who dreams sometimes I know
Of sweetness, sap, and sorcery —
   O, years and years ago!

Life.

Like over-wrought embroideries
   In dainty handicraft embossed,
Producing strange complexities
   In which the true design is lost,
So life a tangled fabric is,
   With threads half-hidden, linked and crossed.

We all are weaving day by day,
   Like ancient, notable housewife,
In our unskilled, imperfect way,
   'Mid cares and disappointments rife,
Rude ells of fretwork to portray
   At last the finished web of life.

But proud success for which we yearn
   Is often hid in trembling doubt;
And when the cause we would discern
   Of hinderance, or threatened rout,
We find that some unlucky turn
   The woof of years has raveled out.

A Gobelin Tapestry.

[Of the time of Louis Quatorze.]

O, had this royal, rich relique —
    This rare *chef-d'œuvre*, odd and old —
Volition, and a tongue to speak,
    What history it might unfold!
'Twould take us back to gilded days
    Of dissolute, imperial France;
When Moliere wrote his classic lays,
    And Fenelon his grand romance.

O, time! how nearly memory fails
    To trace its great antiquity —
Revert to Fontainebleau, Versailles,
    And Louis, lord of luxury!
A sovereign's gift, it may have graced
    The palace home of Maintenon;
Or gratified the cultured taste
    Of connoisseurs, long dead and gone.

It forms the imagery of dreams,
    Invades the Sabbath sanctity,
Disturbs sweet solitude, and seems
    Like some hobgoblin mystery;
The present fades and slips away,
    A panoramic view unrolls
Of lords and ladies, good and gay,
    Or passion-fed, salacious souls.

Then handed down from sire to son
 Along the Bourbon dynasty,
What admiration hath it won
 In many a court festivity!
Perchance it hung behind the throne
 'Mid velvet arras in a scene
Where, like an orient vision, shone
 The fair proportions of a queen.

Was e'er a penny spent in alms
 That this embellished treasure cost —
Per favor dropped within the palms
 That o'er and o'er its meshes crossed?
For hands that could so deftly trace
 A pattern thus complex and quaint,
Might join the ends of raveled lace,
 Or Love's unconscious blushes paint.

Did some poor maid, without renown,
 Toil on the fabric late and long —
Whose pittance bought her wedding gown,
 Its price a sixpence and a song?
Or does it breathe of cloister-cells
 Where pensive virgins, hid for years,
With faces white as immortelles
 Their rosaries told through silent tears?

Or in those far-famed factories,
 Where Gobelin artificers

Knew naught of hard monopolies
  Except as ill-paid laborers,
Was bright young manhood's supple strength
  Through weary seasons robbed of grace,
Embossing one brief cell in length —
  But one that time should not efface?

But why should crowds so frantic be
  Before this antiquated gem —
As 'twere a charm, phylactery,
  Or sort of amulet for them?
Have not our busy dames and belles
  With cunning fingers wrought to-day,
By feminine, spasmodic spells,
  In just as true, artistic way?

Look at our screens and crazy quilts,
  Our lambrequins hung everywhere,
The reptile tribe, or birds on stilts
  That decorate our gay *portieres;*
Embroidered dogs on ottomans,
  So natural that, in the dark,
As faithful household guardians
  They ever serve — but never bark.

O modern art! decry the thought
  That more than we our grandmas knew;
Or that our predecessors caught
  Diviner rays — it isn't true! —

And though in raptures eloquent,
  And rhapsodies we oft engage,
'Tis not o'er skill more excellent —
  But that it bears the stamp of age.

Then, reverend seniors, hear our lay!
  Be not like doleful pessimists,
Lugubrious while growing gray,
  For loving loyalty insists
Upon our honest guarantee;
  'Tis worth the token — be consoled —
For, like this ancient tapestry,
  We'll honor you — because you're old!

Beautiful Eyes.

As clear as lovely Lake Tahoe!
  That, like a mirror's polished face,
  Reveals pure depths where one may trace
The shrubs and flowers that round it grow;
So, as in pantomimic show,
Within their liquid fathoms glow
Quick fancies darting to and fro.

Like opals, changeable to view,
  Their matchless beauty is displayed
  In shifting tints of light and shade;

As if prismatic drops of dew
Had let the golden sunlight through,
And intercepting rays of blue
Took each its own cerulean hue.

Anon they flash like orbs of jet,
  As dark as night, of velvet black;
  And, like a gipsy's, might hurl back
The charge of saucy, gay coquette
From some bewildered amoret;
Then, gray and brown together met,
Grow angel-like in meek regret.

As radiant as diamonds bright
  In exquisite *eadean de noce;*
  A bridal token less verbose,
More pleasing unto sense and sight
Of one upon her marriage-night,
Than tomes of missives pink and white
That loving thought could e'er indite.

A matron's are those love-lit eyes;
  Within whose fringe-encircled spheres
  A soulful, wistful look appears,
That seems to blend, in meaning wise,
The glory and the sweet surprise
Of something seen beyond the skies —
The mystery of Paradise.

Divining-stars! they haunt me so,
 And secrets seem to read as well;
 For things I never meant to tell
To anybody, friend or foe,
Maybe that happened long ago,
Are pictured in them — just as though
Some solemn certainty they know.

A Day in Ancient Rome.

(A Recitation before the Chautauqua Circle.)

Come, let us leave these narrow bounds
 That circumscribe the sphere of home,
And soar away beyond the sea —
 And spend a day in ancient Rome!

In far Italia's sunny land
 Where roll the Arno and the Po,
Where turrets rise from castles grand
 Beside the Tiber's rapid flow.

O, mists of buried years, roll back!
 And bring, in retrospective glance,
The Roman epoch and an age
 That time and distance but enhance.

A few rude shepherds on a hill,
 Their huts and herds, an earthen wall
That hemmed them in from troublous foes —
 Let these the dawn of Rome recall.

Yet, from this petty fortress sprung
  A mighty nation that compelled
All Italy to own her sway,
  And distant peoples subject held ;

That grew in splendor, wealth, and power,
  Became the home of cultured art,
And on the world's arena played
  For centuries the sovereign's part.

Great deities have been dethroned,
  Their thunderbolts are harmless now ;
And so, within their temple walls,
  We stand on Campidoglio's brow,

And cast expectant, rapturous eyes
  Far to the distant Orient —
Where Helios in splendor rose,
  Whose orbit spans the firmament.

Here at our feet the Forum lies,
  Where Cicero with silver tongue
Entranced the wondering populace,
  Who on his thrilling accents hung.

This stony pavement tessellate
  Re-echoed once victorious tread
Of conquering armies from the wars
  Where Caesar, or where Pompey, led.

II — 8

Who laid the trophies of success
    Down at the feet of Jupiter;
For ignorant, blind devotees
    Of heathen gods those ancients were.

On yonder cliff precipitous
    That shadowed the transgressor's gate,
The traitoress, Tarpeia, met
    At Sabine hands her wretched fate.

We tread the Corso's busy street,
    That once triumphal arches spanned;
The Campus Martius wander o'er —
    For promenade aud pleasure planned.

Down through the great Pantheon's dome
    The golden sunlight falls aslant;
Like Heaven's benediction on
    A scene that seraphim might haunt.

Before yon Colosseum's pile
    Might wandering Jews let fall a tear
For captives of their hapeless race
    Compelled those mighty walls to rear.

Oh, were those ruins animate,
    And could their history unfold,
A wondering world would pause to hear
    Their record of the days of old!

We should forget this sordid life,
   Our dearest hopes remember not,
To revel in that glorious past
   With such associations fraught.

The Via Sacra we might walk
   With Horace, our companion-guide —
Or Virgil, whose enchanting lays
   Are our rich legacy and pride.

O, fallen Rome! thy prestige gone,
   Of opulence and splendor shorn,
Till, of thy grandeur, naught remains
   Save fragments — shattered and forlorn.

Thus, proudest monuments upreared
   By man shall yield to slow decay;
The sun shall fade, the stars shall fall,
   Yea, Heaven and earth shall pass away.

When futile things and scenes of time,
   Ephemeral and insecure,
Into oblivion have passed,
   Jehovah and his word endure.

Then what to us if funeral pyre
   Receive our dust, or crumbling sod —
Or where the soul's abode may be,
   If it but safely rest — in God?

"Mad Rose."

(A Seaside Episode.)

Her nose was long, but ended in
    A mighty sudden point;
Not plump, nor plumb above the chin,
    But always out of joint.
Her eyes were serious, dull, and sad;
    Cosmetics made her fair;
I knew all this, but then she had
    The most bewitching hair.
Molasses candy color shone
    In each resplendent braid,
That threw the golden light of sun
    Completely in the shade;
And when in one symmetric coil
    Upon her classic head,
It made the other maidens boil
    With envy — so they said.
As neatly as an artisan
    Might turn a polish-lathe,
I asked her — I, a modest man —
    To go with me — and bathe.
Nay, be not shocked! this etiquette
    Is practised every day
"Down by the sea" — and yet — and yet —
    They're proper — in their way.

A Naiad sojourns in this town
　　Who like a duck can swim,
Or like a tub float upside down,
　　Who boasts — she learned of *him*.
Of course 'twould never do on land,
　　" *Out*-land-ish " it would be —
And this is why, we understand,
　　So many go to sea.
My painted boat at anchor lay,
　　A jaunty craft, but frail,
So, apropos, to close the day
　　We took an evening sail.
A bit of caution going, down,
　　She gave me on the stair :
" Now, Fred ! look out ! if I should drown,
　　Don't grab me by the hair ! "
Her book account eclipsed her nose,
　　She was a " million-heir-
ess ; so I said :　My darling Rose,
　　I'd grab *you* — anywhere ! "
The sky grew dark, the wind arose,
　　The shore lay far beyond ;
Her face was white as her summer-clothes,
　　And mine to correspond.
The boat gave one tremendous pitch,
　　The gale took off her hat —
I never dreamed she wore a switch,
　　And made of jute, at that !
4*

And grappled with despairing force,
　　And sense of urgent need,
At something slippery and coarse
　　Like rope of ocean-weed.
That " mortal coil " came shuffling off,
　　And, wriggling like an eel,
It fell into " the water-trough,"
　　And soon was — *ausgespiel.*
Alas! the pleasure of the day
　　Was marred — and I am sad —
For my unlucky *fiancée*
　　Is bald — and *awful mad!*

The Maker of the Bells.

In that land beyond the sea
　　Where the Pope " a prisoner " dwells,
In a hovel, it may be,
　　Lived the maker of the bells;
Bells that rang in hospices,
　　Called St. Bernard monks to prayer
Or to wandering refugees
　　Spake of rest and shelter there.

Bells resounding through the halls
　　Of the stately Vatican,
Or intoned in cottage-walls
　　Roused the slumbering fisherman;

Bells enshrined in monarchs' homes,
    Trembling like their diadems,
Chiming in cathedral domes,
    Tolling holy requiems.

Oh! the sound of wedding-bells
    Due to his metallic art,
Mingling oft with funeral knells,
    Echoed in his very heart;
Till like friends his bells became,
    He could name them one by one,
Listening by fagot-flame
    When his day of toil was done.

In the belfry-tower of Fame,
    When his masterpiece was placed,
Ruthless the invader came,
    His beloved land laid waste;
Carried to a foreign coast,
    Like a stolen captive bird,
His especial pride and boast —
    Clearer bells were never heard.

Long he sorrowed, like a child
    For a playmate dead and gone,
To his loss unreconciled
    Vain it were to labor on;
So a wanderer he became,
    Drifting to the Emerald isle,

Homeless, hopeless, bent in frame,
　　Never seen or known to smile.

When the clouds of dark despair
　　Hung above him like a pall, .
Sweeter than the voice of prayer,
　　Louder than muezzin-call,
Over Erin's vale and strand,
　　Solemn waves of atmosphere
Bore to him, in anthem grand,
　　Sounds that thrilled his startled ear.

In a moment, as it were,
　　Time and space and grief forgot,
He, the skilled artificer,
　　Glimpses of Italia caught ;
Of his workshop and his home,
　　Children climbing on his knee,
While above St. Peter's dome
　　Rang his chimes across the sea.

Oh ! it seemed that buried years
　　All came back as in a dream,
Smiles were born of happy tears
　　On the banks of Shannon's stream ;
Never music banished pain
　. Like his bells — of life a part ;
But the sudden joyous strain
　　Snapped the tension of his heart.

Adele.

Turn where I may her face I see,
 So beautiful and bright,
One year ago as it looked to me
 Upon her wedding-night;
And it seems so strange that she is gone,
As a star might fade in orient dawn.

Within the sanctuary aisle,
 While music filled the place,
With buoyant step and beaming smile,
 In all her queenly grace
I saw her first, a peerless bride;
A lover's joy, a husband's pride.

Could one of all that brilliant throng,
 This bitter day foresee,
Or know how soon the nuptial song
 A solemn dirge should be,
Or in that festal atmosphere
Discern the shadow of a bier?

Into the dear old church once more
 ·She comes — oh, not as then!
The sad-faced preacher walks before,
 And hands of reverent men
Bear slowly through a weeping crowd
The bride of death — in her snowy shroud.

O Earth! encumbered everywhere
   With dull, unlovely flowers,
Could'st thou not sooner, better spare,
   Than this fair bloom of ours,
Some one that tender look nor word
Compassionate had ever stirred?

The world shall miss her pleasantry,
   And friends her dear caress,
And days and years to come shall be
   So full of weariness;
While cherished hopes in ruins lie,
And cloud-like gloom obscures the sky.

O long as memory shall last,
   'Twill bear on sorrow's wave
A thought of her, with blessings past,
   In motherhood who gave
Herself, a dying sacrifice,
For a stranger soul from Paradise.

Two Questions.

The world perchance may bear in mind
The query: " What is left behind?"
But angels ask, when all is o'er:
" What deeds of good have gone before?"

Western Justice.

'Twas a session of court in an Occident town,
    And the criminal stood in the dock —
The same who had shot a poor Chinaman down —
    With a countenance hard as a rock.

As if to dispel every doubt of his guilt,
    And strengthen the tragic report,
There lay the Celestial whose blood had been spilt,—
    That is, his " remainder " — in court.

The judge, with his sombrero tipped on his head,
    And his pantaloons tucked in his boots,
Was bound to " dispense (*with*) the law," — so he
    " That the present predicament suits."   [said —

The statutes were strict and the chances were slim,
    And well might the law-breaker quail,
When justice, impartial, accorded to him
    A ninety days' sojourn in jail.

" Now, Judge! I'll be hanged—that's a little too steep,
    For surely your honor must know
That the life of a coolie, though ever so cheap,
    Was never so shockingly low."

The man of the ermine betrayed no remorse,
    But read from the page on his knee:
" The minimum — six months for stealing a horse,
    For killing a Chinaman — three! "

The Beautiful Hand.

In thoughtful mood, I sought to trace
　My favorite author's plans,
When suddenly before my face
　Uprose four shapely hands.

Their merry owners, young and fair,
　Purloined my chosen book,
And crowded round my easy-chair
　With eager, wistful look,

And begged for my decision calm,
　To ease their minds distressed;
Which hand before me bore the palm
　Of beauty, o'er the rest.

Divinely, finely-moulded, all
　My admiration drew
To native grace, that might enthrall
　An artist's fancy, too.

Of one I praised the matchless form,
　And its consummate skill,
And clasped another, soft and warm,
　With sweet and tender thrill.

The fairy palm that lay in mine
  Like some pellucid gem,
Might tempt a monarch to resign
  His rightful diadem.

A duchess might have coveted
  Such models plump and small ;
And I, by many fancies led,
  Could not decide at all.

" My dear young friends," I made reply,
  " The fairest, best, most true
In all this world, becomes so by
  The good that it can do."

" They all are beautiful to me,
  And if one does excel
In loveliness, the other three,
  My wisdom cannot tell."

" If, in its honest palm, each day
  Some deed of kindness lives,
Go ask the poor, — and they will say
  ' It is the hand that gives.' "

Parted.

Peace is born of Pain, and we
Say, submissive, "Thy will be!"
Fate has parted you and me.

11—9

To The Stars.

Empyreal lamps, forever bright,
Set in the ebon dome of night
   Like studs of sparkling gold,
What marvels, since Creation's dawn,
Your starry orbs have gazed upon,
   For centuries untold!

Your light shone luminous and warm
Ere Nature rounded into form
   This whirling mundane sphere ;
Ere Luna, with her argent beams,
Bright guardian of a world in dreams,
   Poured forth effulgence clear.

There was a time when sages sought
To win, by ceaseless toil and thought,
   The secrets of the skies ;
To read the destinies of man,
And fathom God's mysterious plan,
   Concealed from mortal eyes.

Oh, later Science laughs to scorn,
As idle superstition, born
   Of ignorance profound,
The ancient astrologic art,
Which swayed the seer's prophetic heart,
   And made him world-renowned.

Great prophets, once accounted wise,
With straining orbs who searched the skies,
   Your plan excites our mirth ;
For we, with lengthened tube of brass
And double lens of convex glass,
   Bring down the stars to earth.

                HARRY HOWARD.

A Noted Place.

A picture hangs upon my wall
That fascinates the gaze of all ;
   It is no dream of fancy,
The reveling of fond conceit
In some fantastic brain replete
   With wild extravagancy.

Nor he who dared the scene to limn
Could so have wrought from idle whim,
   But, as by inspiration ;
And gave to common things the glow
That angel fingers might bestow
   On some divine creation.

Who seized the palette of the skies,
And dipped his brush in Eden dyes,
   And caught the sunset glory,
To represent — a waterfall

As issuing from a ragged wall
Of rock with cycles hoary.

A deep ravine, o'ershadowed by
Huge precipices mountain high ;
    That stand, as cleft asunder,
Like bold gigantic sentinels
To guard the loveliest of dells,
    And Nature's rarest wonder.

A streamlet bent like a shepherd's crook,
Defining many a cozy nook,
    Within whose sweet seclusion
May weary toilers, care-distressed,
Enraptured linger, dream, and rest;
    Secure from rude intrusion.

Where cunning elves, in sportive freak,
Might play at charming " hide and seek "
    Till, echoing long after,
Should hill and dale return the sound
Of wild hilarity's rebound,
    In peals of spirit-laughter.

Might not the amatory Muse
Who in her dainty chalice brews
    The wine of fond desire —
The lovely rose-crowned Erato,
In these recesses long ago
    Have tuned her magic lyre ?

Whose dulcet strains inspire still,
And touch with Passion's tender thrill,
  The scores of youthful lovers
That here, in some sequestered spot,
Remembering each — the world forgot —
  One everywhere discovers.

Oh motley crowds of visitors,
As artists, tramps, philosophers,
  The place are ever haunting;
So oft described by tongue and pen
That all the world knows "Watkins' Glen"
  Is perfectly enchanting.

Inn-Hospitality.

Within a spacious corridor,
A waiter found a visitor,
His visage drawn into a knot
With mortal rage, because he thought
  The management had tricked him;
" Are you a guest of this hotel?"
Asked the white-aproned Afric swell.
  " A guest! No, I'm a victim!"

HARRY HOWARD.

9*

Loved and Lost.

O it was sad to bear her
    (That chill November night)
Away from all who loved her so,
    Away from life and light;
To hollow a grave in the frozen mold,
And leave her alone in the dark and cold.

As if the dress that robed her
    Like shining nebulae,
When marriage-vows unclosed her lips,
    Now folded rigidly,
And pillows soft her cheeks that press
Could give her warmth's luxuriousness.

O could a ray of sunshine,
    To cheer the long, long hours,
Have struggled through the casket-lid
    With all its wealth of flowers,
And through the satin and the lace,
The iciness 'twould half displace.

Or had it been that morning's
    Delicious light and air
Had bathed her grave a little while,
    Before we laid her there,
We could have turned away with less
Regret, and more of hopefulness.

If day's meridian splendor
  Had fallen on her face,
When tearfully we laid her in
  Her lowly dwelling-place,
It would have seemed in loving thought
A golden halo round the spot.

Upon the solemn midnight,
  From hearts unreconciled,
Goes out the pleading anguish-cry,
  Despairing, sad, and wild:
" Beloved, from that unseen shore
  Come back, come back to us once more."

O heaven must be brighter
  For one like summer's rose
Who perished in her loveliness,
  And sleeps beneath the snows ;
But, in immortal grace and bloom,
Who lives again beyond the tomb.

Our Fault.

If never in our skies appear
Refulgent gleams the heart to cheer,
  And make the sombre world aglow;
If Life is always dull and drear,
  'Tis just because we make it so.

"The Mind Cure."

Oh, who knows what the "mind cure" is?
The "latest craze" in remedies
  That everybody's trying —
For if the rumors half be true
Of all that it is said to do,
  'Twill save a world of dying.

"The age of miracles is past!
A nine-days' wonder — 'twill not last!"
  So says the horrid skeptic;
But, on the other hand, we find
A host of maimed, and halt, and blind,
  Consumptive and dyspeptic,

Of rich and poor, of high and low,
Who've tried it, and who ought to know,
  Declare there's virtue in it;
They say it beats their puzzled brains
How it can banish ills and pains,
  In less than half a minute.

It takes a "crank," as full of kinks
As a wire-mattress is of links,
  With aching joints rheumatic,
And straightens every tangle out;
And makes him run and leap and shout
  In sudden joy ecstatic.

Suppose a stomach's knotted up
Until it can't retain a sup
   Of anything (but whisky),
Just seek the " mind-magician's " haunt,
He says, " Eat anything you want!"
   Is not this rather risky?

A pair of squinting, crooked eyes
That never saw the azure skies
   But as a cross-barred vision,
With one unbias'd, air-line glance
Straightway transforms the broad expanse
   Into a scene Elysian.

They say a twisted, curved back-bone.
That like the letter S has grown,
   Can be a thing of beauty ;
Each vertebra its place slip in,
Without a drop of medicine —
   But just from sense of duty.

Now, this is certainly benign!
For who could live without a spine —
   A reservoir for marrow?
The plan should anybody try,
He very soon would occupy
   A space secure — but narrow.

Old fogy doctors of the town
Would dearly love to put it down,
    As humbug — for the fact is,
They find "their occupation's gone,"
As patients everywhere are drawn
    To this new-fangled practice.

A journal, too, renowned and wise,
The noble " mind-cure " classifies
    With modern " shams, delusions."
With " woman suffrage, come-out schemes "
Of some fanatic's phantom dreams —
    Oh, what absurd conclusions !

We don't see why an editor
Should ever cast a harmless slur
    On innocent diversions;
But greatly fear — the thought is sad —
That "too much learning makes him mad,"
    And fond of mild aspersions.

What does the " mind-cure doctor " do ?
Why, not a thing but look at you,
    As if he were enchanted ;
And presently, your stubborn will
Is conquered by his little (?) bill,
    Which in your face is flaunted.

O matchless "mind-cure" mystery!
Let not the bond of faith in thee
  A ruthless hand dissever;
For they who once thy name maligned,
Are "sitting, clothed, in their right mind,"
  And hope to live — forever.

O Wear a Smiling Face.

O wear a smiling face,
  No matter what your sorrow!
Let not the doleful trace
Of private woes displace
The sunny glance, nor chase
  Bright hours into the morrow!

And speak a cheerful word,
  E'en though your heart be breaking!
Like happy song of bird,
It may revive when heard
Some drooping spirit, stirred
  To depths of bitter aching.

It is not ours to know
  How oft a nobler yearning,
In some sad life below,
Is born of that sweet glow
The countenance doth show
  With love-light ever burning.

A Christmas Fowl.

Five mortal hours I cooked that chicken,
  And then sat down and cried;
For when a fork I tried to stick in,
  It never pierced its hide. .

A tougher biped strutted never
  Upon a barn-yard plain;
I'd like to wring its neck forever,
  And would, if I had it again.

I put in soda, salt and savor-
  y stuff, till nearly dark,
To reconstruct that ancient flavor,
  That smelt like Noah's ark.

And waited — I, a starving sinner —
  Till six o'clock at night;
And ordered, long before the dinner,
  The paraffine — for light.

I half-expired, no longer able
  To bear such emptiness;
And just revived when to the table
  It came — in evening dress.

But when the platter took its form on
  Its horrid eye-teeth showed;
And just as true as I'm a Mormon,
  That chicken got up and crowed.

www.ingramcontent.com/pod-product-compliance
Lightning Source LLC
Chambersburg PA
CBHW030550270326
41927CB00008B/1585